To Glenna and Ed,

FINDING HOPE

a journey of faith through uncertain times

God bless you!
Love, Dick & Kathy

Lynelle Watford

Rising Higher Series

D1519269

This collection of thoughts and selected Scriptures is best read with contemplation. Let the words, like a slow rain, soak deep into your soul.

You may not have rheumatoid arthritis, serious eyesight challenges, or the grief of losing a son to suicide as I do, but these Scriptures can minister to your heart as they do min.

Lynelle Watford

Finding Hope: a journey of faith through uncertain times
Copyright © 2019 by Lynelle Watford. All rights reserved.

ISBN-9781796908190

Cover: Photo by Todd Trapani on Unsplash, Design by Lynelle Watford and Wayne Watford. Editing by Nancy Rooker. Proofreading by Lila Chandler.

© 2019 Rising Higher ~ Praise Song:
Words by Lynelle Watford; Music by Michaela Smith & Kent Wade. All Rights Reserved.

Unless otherwise indicated, all Scripture quotations are from the ESV Bible (The Holy Bible, English Standard Version) copyright 2001 by Crossway, a publishing ministry of Good News Publishers. Used by permission. All rights reserved.

The Bible in Basic English (BBE), printed in 1965 by Cambridge Press, England. Public domain.

GOD'S WORD (GW) is a copyrighted work of God's Word to the Nations. Quotations are used by permission. Copyright 1995 by God's Word to the Nations. All rights reserved.

Greene's Literal Translation of the Holy Bible (LITV), 1985, by Jay P. Greene, Sovereign Grace Publishers.

Net proceeds from the sale of this book will be donated to the support of orphans through GlobalFingerprints.

Vistas

I was mesmerized. Narrow gauge train tracks rolled out beneath my feet as I stood on the train's observation platform.

Mile after mile, sometimes curving around a mountain, sometimes straight across a meadow. A picture of life.

Sometimes we think we know what lies ahead.

But at times we can't imagine the future—or don't want to. Clues—a cancer diagnosis, a spouse's suspected unfaithfulness, an employer's tightening budget—warn us we may be headed to the dark side of a mountain. Or over its edge.

Join me as we ponder a collection of assorted truths that sustain me in uncertain times.

Together, we'll find hope.

Calamities & Confessions

Are you in unwanted circumstances? I am.

I can't see far down the 'train tracks' of life, but I know enough. Diminishing vision with no clear diagnosis and no treatment. The trends in our culture for dim lighting push my fear and discomfort buttons.

I can't change the dim lighting in public places, but I can allow change in my life. It's more than today's struggles though, it's ...

In the unknown. How will I cook when I can't measure ingredients?

In the losses. How will I read to my grandchildren when I can't make out the words on the page?

In the fears. How will I survive if something happens to my husband?

It's the thousand points of frustration every day.

This could get ugly. Unless. Unless, God does a work in me.

First, I need to see my need and tell God about it. Would you join me?

Prayer
God, I am needy.
I can't see my way
through this mess.
I feel like falling apart.
So, I lay it all before You—
the unknown, the losses,
the fears, the frustrations.

I know
You are enough.

Goodness on Display

God is good. Like a traveler to a compass, I cling to this truth.

But sometimes I have doubts. After all, what is good about suffering, loss, and all the broken things in a fallen world?

Apart from God—nothing.

In Psalm 31, David rehearses his anguish over his troubles while affirming his trust in a good God. As he concludes his complaints, verse 19 erupts like sunshine through clouds, expressing overwhelming amazement in God's goodness:

> *Oh, how abundant is your goodness, which you have stored up for those who fear you and worked for those who take refuge in you, in the sight of the children of mankind!*

After 18 verses of pouring out his deep brokenness while imploring God's help, how could the psalmist break out in praise?

As he ends the psalm, he confesses that it is in times of great need that the Lord hears and protects. The psalmist realizes it is the trials that highlight God's goodness, love, and power.

Our trials

highlight

God's

goodness,

love,

and

power.

Oh, how abundant is your goodness,
… for those who take refuge in you!
In the cover of your presence
you hide them …
you store them in your shelter …

Psalm 31:19-20

God Is Holding Me

Joy can grow
in the deepest valley,
praise can rise
in the darkest night.

Peace can reign
in the wildest tempest,
for God
is holding me tight.

Hope can bloom
in the driest desert,
faith can soar
in the dreariest day.

Grace can rule
when strength has languished,
for God
keeps all of my ways.

Unexpected Faces of Love

Have you ever sensed God whispering, "Let me love you?"

In our rushed, distracted lives, it's easy to overlook God's love.

Several years ago, I noticed His love in an unexpected way and wrote about it in my journal:

> Today it rained. I hadn't felt well for days, and I got behind a slow car. Earlier, the words God might say to me, "Let Me love you," had been on my mind.

> Could the plodding of the car in front of me that caused me to slow down be an evidence of God's love? For by forcing me to slow down, I was made more aware of my desperate need for God and how unfulfilling lesser things are.

Might the pains,
complications,
frustrations,
and grief of life
that slow you down
become an expression
of God's love?

Be intentional about noticing
the many tiny evidences
of God's love
strewn throughout your days.

Let Me Love You

Let Me love you.
Open your eyes
to see it raining down.

Let Me love you.
Inside, outside, and all around.

When you walk
through times of darkness
My love is slowing you down,
gently pulling you into My arms
right where My love
can be found.

When life's strains
and stresses tire you
My love beckons you come,
into My refreshing presence
right where love
can be found.

Let Me love you.
Open your eyes
to see it raining down.

Let Me love you.
Inside, outside, and all around.

"I have
loved you
with an
everlasting love!

With
loving-kindness
I have drawn you.

Jeremiah 31:3 LITV

Perspective Walk

Some enjoy combing Lake Michigan's shore for beach glass. One woman calls her return trip her 'perspective walk.' As she sees the shoreline with the sunlight shining from a different angle, she often finds bits of beach glass she missed earlier.

She finds treasure where once she saw only sand.

Perspective is essential.

When I imagine the challenges that I may face with continuing loss of vision, I shudder.

But if I consider my loss in relation to eternity, the dark, looming mountain shrinks to a grain of golden sand. Ten to twenty years of challenges will be nothing compared to eternity, when my eyes will be healed.

In the end, our earthly perspective results in disappointment and despair, fear and frustration. Looking from God's perspective—an eternal perspective—through His Word, results in joy and hope, trust and tranquility. Even when life is falling apart.

Let the light of God's Word reveal the treasure in your path.

We look not

to the things

that are *seen*

but to the things

that are *unseen*.

For the things that

are seen

are *transient,*

but the things that

are unseen

are *eternal.*

2 Corinthians 4:18

Come to me,
all you who are
troubled and
weighted down with care,
and I will give you
rest.

Matthew 11:28 BBE

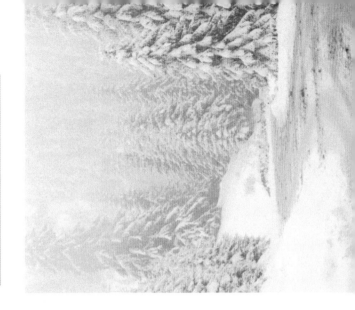

> *When we praise God, our troubles shrink.*
>
> *God's goodness and sufficiency are magnified.*

Take a Break

Life is hard. Especially in uncertain times. Sometimes we need a break from our burdens.

God understands. (*Blessed be the God and Father ... of all comfort, who comforts us in all our affliction ...* 2 Corinthians 1:3-4).

He longs for us to find moments of relief and comfort, not in things that harm us, but in His healing presence.

What better way of entering His presence than through praise? Praising God and focusing on truth puts everything in perspective. Our troubles shrink. God's goodness and sufficiency are magnified.

Rising Higher: Praise Song

On the wings of the wind, on the very breath of God
we rise ever higher to You.
Leaving our cares behind, we're uplifted by Your rest
we give all praise to You, we give all praise to You.

As my flesh begins to fade like the beauty of the flower
I rise ever higher to You.
As my weakness falls away and I trust in Your power
I give all praise to You, I give all praise to You.

And each voice shall cry out and every eye shall behold
the glory of the Lord, the glory of the Lord.

(Listen to this song at ForeverWaters.com/gift-books)

All flesh is grass, and all its beauty
is like the flower of the field.
The grass withers, the flower fades,
but the word of our God will
stand forever.

Isaiah 40:6, 8

Value Weakness

We are weak. Always have been. Even when we think we rule the world by the tail. Any strength we think we have, apart from God, is an illusion.

When circumstances convince our souls of our weakness, they are a gift. Our sense of fragility helps us appreciate God's power and sufficiency.

The Lord is my light
and my salvation;
whom shall I fear?

The Lord is the stronghold
of my life;
of whom shall I be afraid?

Psalm 27:1

But I trust in you, O LORD; I say, "You are my God." Psalm 31:14

You Are My Strength

You give strength to face the day ...

... when the tsunami of sorrow, the terrors of troubles
threaten to erode the foundations of my life.

... when confusion and conflicts consume my waking moments,
steal my peace and confidence in You.

... when I need protection from myself, from my fears,
from the darkness that desires to conquer me.

For You alone
are my strength.

No one else
loves enough
is strong enough
to be that tower
that fortress.

You, and You alone
are the one
I will trust.

Let the
Light of Christ
surround you.

Reach for the Light

Exhale
the problems
of your heart
buried deep within.

Breathe deeply
of faith in Christ
the Eternal Lord.

Let the ashes
of today
swirl up
and
fly away
with the wind.

Let the light
of the one
whose days
will never end
surround you.

"Let not your hearts
be troubled....

If I go and prepare
a place for you,
I will come again
and will take you
to myself,
that where I am
you may be also."

John 14:1, 3

Remember & Resolve

"You have beautiful hands."

I didn't know what to say. A seasoned shopkeeper in a tiny Colorado mountain town was telling me I had beautiful hands.

In my more confident moments, I can imagine God saying those words. For God sees beyond my gnarly fingers and rheumatoid nodules.

But who would see—and a stranger at that—beyond the abnormalities to the life God has birthed through years of suffering?

"I've had rheumatoid arthritis for almost 50 years," I explained. "God has used it to do a beautiful work in my life."

Her kind words echoed in my heart. A compelling reminder that God has done something grace-filled through past losses and pain. An on-going lesson to rehearse God's faithfulness.

He can do the same amazing work through your challenges today.

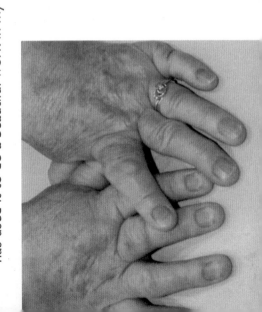

"Man looks on the outward appearance,
but the LORD looks on the heart."

I Samuel 16:7

Have a Plan

Do you have a plan when you shop for groceries? Take a trip? Start a big project? Probably.

Do you have a plan for your thoughts? You talk to yourself more than anyone else. What you say is crucial!

Focus on God's truth. Why? The Word will help keep you in constant communion with God's thoughts and ways. Truth will counteract untrue thoughts. You will see life from God's perspective.

Use your moments when your mind is inactive to reflect on scripture. Memorize verses—one or many—to use for meditation. Even one short phrase a day will accomplish the purpose.

Set your mind up to stay on track and keep moving forward!

> Whatever is true
> whatever is honorable, whatever is just,
> whatever is pure, whatever is lovely ...
> think about these things.
>
> Philippians 4:8

> When you pass
> through the waters,
> I will be with you ...
> you are precious
> in my eyes,
> and honored,
> and I love you.
> Fear not,
> for I am with you;
>
> Isaiah 43:2, 4, 5

Always with Us

In bed one night, tears rolled down my cheeks as I thought about our younger son lost to suicide nearly eight years earlier.

Diverting my attention, I began reviewing a recently memorized scripture passage. As I did, my reflections turned to our newborn granddaughter, first with happy thoughts, then sad. *She will surely face hardships in life.*

Still, the truths in Isaiah 43 encouraged me. The Lord will be with her through the hard times. The lullaby I wrote for Avelyn may comfort those of any age.

Avelyn's Lullaby

Fear not, little one
for the Lord
is with you.

He calls you by name
and will carry
you through ...

Through the
hard times of life
though they may
bring a tear.

Fear not, little one
He is near.

Like a *shepherd*
he *takes care* of his flock.
He *carries* them in his arms.

Isaiah 40:11 God's Word

Rest in Him

The same God
who measures
the waters of the sea
in the palm of His hand
and marks off the sky
with the length of His fingers,
takes care of you, His child.

The same God
who gathers
the dust of the earth
in a bushel basket
and weighs the mountains on
scales and hills on a balance,
carries you close
when you are weak.

Rest in Him.

God is both infinite
and intimate ...
rest in Him.

Security

"I don't feel like God is a refuge," I lamented. "Every time I get in this particular situation, I feel afraid, as though I'm losing control."

Neither my friend's sympathy nor quoting Psalm 46:1 gave me the confidence that God is my refuge.

Perhaps the problem is that I've made other things my security, such as certain people and my abilities. When those people are gone and I can no longer perform, I believe my value as a person is at risk.

No matter how I feel, Psalm 46 declares that God is a refuge, ready to help. Because He is there, I will not be shaken; I will not fall if I am clinging to Him.

When we are ready to leave the crumbling securities of our lives, God will still be there with open arms. Faithful. Unshakable. Secure.

By Your power I am fastened
to the Rock that stands secure.

Though the storms blow round about me
I find safety in Your arms.

You stay ever right beside me, attentive to my needs
though I'm weak and truly needy, You want to be with me
You want to be with me.

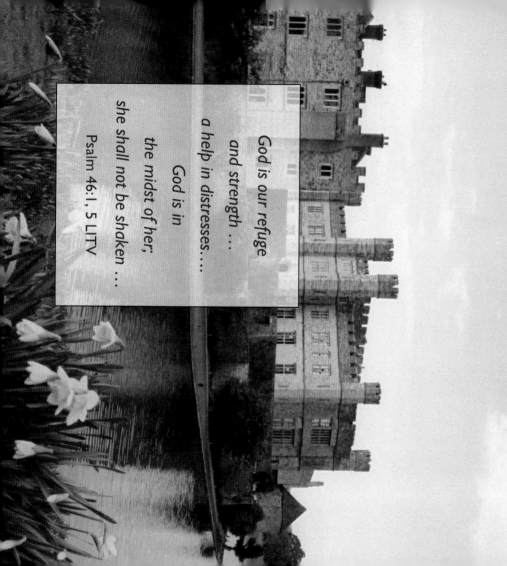

God is our refuge
and strength …
a help in distresses….

God is in
the midst of her;
she shall not be shaken …

Psalm 46:1, 5 LITV

"My grace
is sufficient for you,
for my power
is made perfect
in weakness."

2 Corinthians 12:9

Invite God's Grace

One summer we vacationed on Spider Lake. Despite the lake's murkiness, I determined to get some water exercise.

I waded in. Even with my water shoes, I could sense the slime of vegetation beneath my feet and feel it clinging to my ankles. What else lay hidden beneath the surface?

I swam to the diving platform, but my apprehension only increased. Choking fear nearly drove me back to shore.

Uncertainty. Murkiness. Worry.

Something may be wrong—altogether wrong—but we can't be sure because we can't see into the future. It may be financial, relational, or medical.

The unknown smothers.

Unlike my Spider Lake experience, we are powerless to leave.

Though you can't change the situation, you can invite God's grace and strength into your life.

Admit your need, your brokenness. God will pour His grace—the desire and power to live according to His ways—into your life.

Though you can't change the situation, you can invite God's grace into your life.

The most painful
and deepest hurts
can become the clearest
and sweetest
wells of God's grace
and joy.

Prayer

Lord, I fear what I see, and I fear the unseen.
I don't want to make this journey without You.
Blanket my needy heart with the strength of Your grace.
May all my moments bring glory to You.

If you enjoyed this book, please leave a review at Amazon.com. Your review will help more people find encouragement through this book. Thank you.

Topics in this book:

Calamities & Confessions, Goodness on Display, Unexpected Faces of Love, Perspective Walk, Take a Break, Value Weakness, Reach for the Light, Remember and Resolve, Have a Plan, Always with Us, Rest in Him, Security, Invite God's Grace

Other books in the Rising Higher series:

Never Alone: gentle reminders of God's presence and love
After Loss: courage and healing through God's grace

More books by Lynelle Watford are available at ForeverWaters.com:

Out of the Ashes: Hope
Out of the Desert: Refreshment
Out of the Storm: Peace
Waters of Refreshment
Soul Pursuit: The Busy Person's Guide to Biblical Meditation

Connect with Lynelle Watford and subscribe to her blog at ForeverWaters.com.

Made in the USA
Columbia, SC
18 November 2020

24829700R00024